Patterns of Infinity

Where All the Numbers Come From

Tony Butcher

Grosvenor House
Publishing Limited

This book is published by
Grosvenor House Publishing Ltd
Link House
140 The Broadway, Tolworth, Surrey, KT6 7HT.
www.grosvenorhousepublishing.co.uk

A CIP record for this book
is available from the British Library

ISBN 978-1-83975-316-9

Mathematics is often called the Science of Patterns.

"A mathematician, like a painter or a poet, is a maker of patterns.   If his patterns are more permanent than theirs, it is because they are made with ideas" (Hardy, 1992, p. 84)

L.A. Steen said " Mathematics has become the Science of Patterns. In mathematics the primary subject-matter is not the individual mathematical objects, but rather the structures in which they are arranged" (Resnik, 1999, p.201).

"The word pattern denotes a sense of order and regularity and lawfulness that gives rise to what we see and perceive in the external world". (Keith Devlin)

"...in mathematics the primary subject-matter is not the individual mathematical objects but rather the structures in which they are arranged." (Resnik, 1999, p.201)

"The entire field of mathematics is the Science of Patterns and any sequence of numbers in mathematics has a pattern. At its source the pattern is repeated to generate it on a larger scale." (Wille, 2010)

"Mathematics is regarded as our most developed science, and yet philosophical troubles surface as soon as we inquire about its subject matter partly because mathematics itself says nothing about the metaphysical nature of its objects." (Michael Resnik)

"Where there is life there is a pattern, and where there is a pattern there is mathematics." (John D. Barrow)

"Nature is the realisation of the simplest conceivable mathematical ideas." (Einstein)

"Mathematics possesses not only truth but supreme beauty." (Bertrand Russell)

Contents

Key:

Learning Points

Practice Page

Preface

I have developed a new method which could revolutionise the way times-tables are taught in schools. Rather than using the old-fashioned learn by rote method; a system unpopular with many pupils, this method uses the ancient Japanese system of multiplication, allowing the child a visual aid to find the answer to any particular pair of numbers by drawing two sets of diagonal lines.

Once an individual table is established and in front of them, the child will be shown how to identify and pattern the recurring sequence of numbers from two distinct code in both the units and tens columns.

I think Primary aged children and some Secondary pupils who find rote-learning a pain will find it a little more visually interesting and a much easier way to learn their tables.

Patterns of Infinity

Where all the Numbers Come From

One of the best kept secrets that most people don't know about is that Multiplication Tables actually have at least two hidden codes, which makes them both interesting and easy to learn.

Nature has a pattern. Everything comes out of a round zero shape. Just as chicks come out of eggs and plants and trees grow out of seeds, numbers come out of a big zero, which scientists call the Unified Field.

There are only ten numbers including the nought or zero. Sometimes we call them figures but they are both the same thing.

Often we only talk about only nine of them because the nought or zero is only used to show that there is nothing to count but that is the wrong way to look at it. It is actually the most important because it is both the Mother and Father of all the others. All of the numbers come out of it, as well as everything else. Without it, we could only go up to nine and go no further. It is due to the nought or zero that we are able to count at all. The zero is the magic number that allows numbers to go on forever; past tens, hundreds, thousands and millions.

As there are only nine numbers, no matter how large the number is, if you add up all the figures in it as single numbers, we end up with one of them. Take 43 for example. If we add the 4 in the Tens column to the 3 in the Units column we get 7. This is the clue we use to work out the tens column in some of the tables.

Odd and Even Numbers

Except for the first- number 1 - which is in every number, numbers come in two very different forms. They are normally called 'odd' and 'even'. By 'odd' we don't mean strange or unusual. Just like boys and girls they are different from each other. Even numbers look more balanced and have the same number of dots on both sides like 2 ••, 4 ••••, 6 •••••• and 8 ••••••••, but odd numbers like 3 •••, 5 ••••••, 7 ••••••• and 9 ••••••••• have an extra dot in the middle.

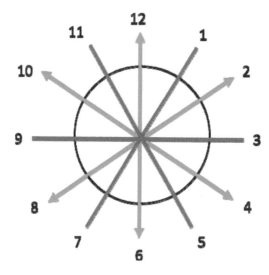

The even numbers are: 0 2 4 6 8 10 12

And the odd ones are: 1 3 5 7 9 11

Take out two of your favourite colours. Have one for the even numbers and the other for the odd numbers.

Colour the pattern below

1	2	3	4	5	6	7	8	9	10	11	12
2	4	6	8	10	12	14	16	18	20	22	24
3	6	9	12	15	18	21	24	27	30	33	36
4	8	12	16	20	24	28	32	36	40	44	48

2

Music and numbers are like brothers and sisters. They both like forming patterns that keep on repeating, like the chorus of a song.

That is why I have called this 'Patterns of Infinity'.

This is a picture of infinity. It is like a figure eight lying on its side. The important thing about it is that goes on forever and never stops. If you put your finger in the middle and follow the line around you will find it will soon be on the other side and back. There is no place to stop. In much the same way as your finger went from one side to the other, each table has a pattern of numbers in the units column which keep coming back and helps you to get the right answer. You will be helped to find the pattern for each table by using an easy way of multiplying that children use in Japan.

We will start off most of the tables and work up to 9 or 10. We will do these first and finish them later on in the book. Then we will also learn how to multiply larger numbers like 11 , 12 and more.

The Multiplication Sign

Multiplication is really a quick way of adding. The sign between the numbers is an 'X' like the shape you see in a sword battle.

It is an ancient system, believed to have been created in India. It is still used today in Japan to teach multiplication to children and it is a great method to use to for multiplication as it is based on such a simple (sword) cross and count method.

Let's start by looking at :   1   X   1 =

If we cross 1 straw (or 1 sword) with another 1 straw (or 1 sword) it will look like this:

We will then see that the two straws only cross over at one point – they just cross once - so the answer is: 1   X   1 = 1

Now let's just go back a small step and look at 1 x 0 and what that could equal when we use this method. Well, there is only one straw multiplied by no other so there is nothing to make a cross so the answer must also be nothing – no points where the straws cross.

1 X 0 = 0

Now let's go forward a small step and look at how we could work out 2 X 0

As before, you lay down the first part of the sum which is 2 (so 2 straws) and then you have zero straws to multiply them by so there is no cross these, so 2 X 0 = 0

In fact, anything multiplied by 0 is always 0.

The Two Times Table

Using your newly learned Japanese method can you now count up the circled crosses of each one of the diagrams below? These images show us crossing lines represented by each side of the sum.

1 X 2 =

Pretend the lines are the straws we have just used and let's make our own 2 times table by counting the crosses and putting the answers beside each equals sign.

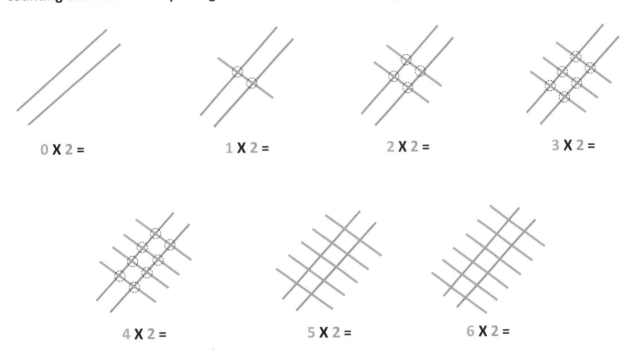

0 X 2 =   1 X 2 =   2 X 2 =   3 X 2 =

4 X 2 =   5 X 2 =   6 X 2 =

Can you see how many sword fights ╳ are being fought at 4x2? All we do is count up the number of crosses. I have circled them for you. You can either do the rest yourself or just count how many times the lines cross.

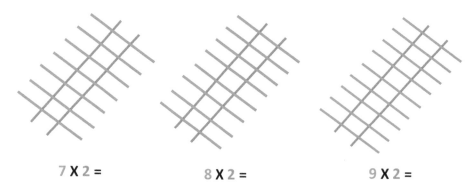

7 X 2 =   8 X 2 =   9 X 2 =

We will now look at some examples of the way that we could learn the 2 times table.

As everything comes out of the big zero we will put it first: 0   2   4   6 and 8   and keeps repeating. Look at the last figures in the Two Times Table

0 X 2 = 0

1 X 2 = 2

2 X 2 = 4

3 X 2 = 6

4 X 2 = 8

5 X 2 =

6 X 2 =

7 X 2 =

8 X 2 =

9 X 2 =

A good way to remember this code is to use your hand. Think of your thumb as the zero, the first finger the 2 and the middle finger 4. The ring finger becomes a 6 and the little finger an 8. Now close your hand and open it up one at a time saying 0, 2, 4, 6, 8. Do this a few times and you will always remember it.

You will see that 0 2 4 6 8 keep repeating. Tables usually only go up to 12 but if we went a little further- what would we see?

		T	U
10 X 2 = 20		2	0
11 X 2 = 22		2	2
12 X 2 = 24		2	4
13 X 2 = 26		2	6
14 X 2 = 28		2	8
15 X 2 = 30		3	0

Although the numbers get bigger, the pattern of 0, 2, 4, 6 and 8 keeps on repeating in the units column forever.

If that's not enough there is another way to help us learn this table. It is a pattern that gives rise to the tens column. We get this by adding the numbers of both the tens column and the units column together.

I know this is something we must never do when we are doing our sums in class. What we are doing here is learning where the numbers come from.

The first five: 0 2 4 6 8 stay as they are because there are no tens in them.

The next five are : 10, 12, 14, 16, 18

If we add up the two figures of ten we get 1 + 0 = 1

If we do the same for: 1 + 2 =   1 + 4 =   1 + 6 =   1 + 8 =

We get the odd number pattern of : 1   3   5   7   9

If we went on a bit further- what would we find? More patterns!

10 X 2 = 20	2 + 0 = 2
11 X 2 = 22	2 + 2 = 4
12 X 2 = 24	2 + 4 = 6
13 X 2 = 26	2 + 6 = 8
14 X 2 = 28	2 + 8 = 10 and 1 + 0 = 1

This time we have a pattern for the even numbers, including the last, which is the beginning of the next odd number sequence.

If you think I am kidding let's look at a few more patterns:

15 X 2 = 30	3 + 0 =
16 X 2 = 32	3 + 2 =
17 X 2 = 34	3 + 4 =
18 X 2 = 36	3 + 6 =

Looking back at all the numbers in the two times table-what do you notice?

That's right! The even number pattern of 0 2 4 6 8 comes first but forms the units column and then the odd number pattern of 1 3 5 7 9 comes next to help work out the tens column before the units.

If we remember the two sets of numbers we could easily create the whole table.

We already know the units column. Now we will see how the odd number pattern helps us to finish off the table.

As there are no tens in the first five numbers we will begin when the pattern begins again with ten. Ten is made up of two numbers: 1 and 0. Add them together and we get 1.

The next is twelve. Add up the 1 and the 2 and we get 3.

Which two numbers add up to 5 ..... 1 and 4 and so on until the even numbers kick in again.

It is best to fill in the Units column first and leave a space to put in the Tens column later:

$$0 \times 2 =$$
$$1 \times 2 =$$
$$2 \times 2 =$$
$$3 \times 2 =$$
$$4 \times 2 =$$
$$5 \times 2 =$$
$$6 \times 2 =$$
$$7 \times 2 =$$
$$8 \times 2 =$$
$$9 \times 2 =$$
$$10 \times 2 =$$

This is the way we will do all the even number tables.

I have left out the last two for the time being.

Let's do a few more to help you remember. You may find it easier to draw the lines for each numbers and count how many times they cross. When you draw them, think of the number on a clock. The lines for the table itself goes from 8 to 2 and how many from 10 to 4.

Another way is to use your other hand. Your first hand gives you the last figure up to 4 the other hand will help you with the rest. Imagine you get stuck on 7 X 2. 7 is just three more so the middle figure of your other hand will let you know it is 4

Revision

Remember the units column is 0 2 4 6 8 on your hands. There are no tens for numbers 0 – 4 times and only one ten for 5 – 9 times and 2 for 10 times.

5 X 2 =   7 X 2 =   2 X 2 =   10 x 2 =   8 X 2 =

6 X 2 =   1 X 2 =   9 X 2 =   0 X 2 =   3 X 2 =

4 X 2 =   9 X 2 =   7 X 2 =   6 X 2 =   8 X 2 =

Now turn to the back of the book to mark your answers and see how many you got right … celebrate your success!

The Four Times Table

Let's stay with the even numbers so we get used to doing things this way.

Lets look at the 4 times table.

We will start the Japanese way to get the pattern of numbers for the first five answers units of this table by filling in the answers below.

0 X 4 =

1 X 4 =

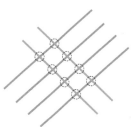

2 X 4 =

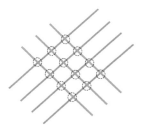

3 X 4 =

4 X 4 =

5 X 4 =

Fill in the answers to:

0   X   4 =

1   X   4 =

2   X   4 =

3   X   4 =

4   X   4 =

1 3

Just like the 2 times table the four times table uses the same five numbers to repeat in a slightly different pattern of: 0 4 8 2 and 6:

This time make your thumb the zero, the first finger 4. The middle finger 8. The ring finger 2 and the little finger 6. Now close your hand and open it up one at a time saying 0, 4, 8, 2 and 6. Do this several times.

Now we will do the same for the next five and write the answers to see the pattern easily.

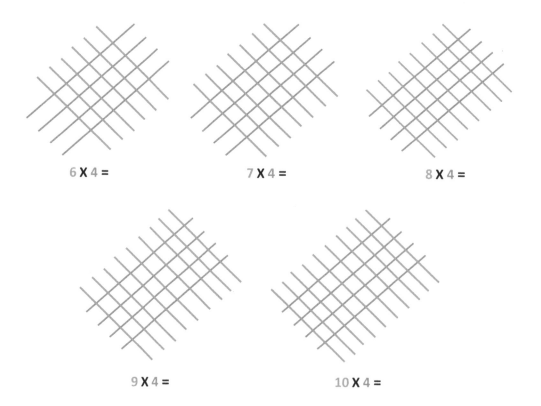

6 X 4 =   7 X 4 =   8 X 4 =

9 X 4 =   10 X 4 =

Put in all of your answers of the units column in the table below up to 10 X 4=40.

Don't forget to leave a space in front to make room for the tens column number:

	U	
0 X 4 = 0	0	5 X 4 = 20
1 X 4 = 4	4	6 X 4 = ...4
2 X 4 = 8		7 X 4 = ...8
3 X 4 = 12		8 X 4 = ...2
4 X 4 = 16		9 X 4 = ...6
		10 X 4 = ... 0

Now we will find the code or pattern which gives rise to those numbers.

You fill in the rest:

0 X 4 = 0

1 X 4 = 4

2 X 4 = 8

3 X 4 = 12

4 X 4 = 16

5 X 4 = 20

6 X 4 = ...4

7 X 4 = ...8

8 X 4 = ...2

9 X 4 = ...6

10 X 4 = ...0

Now we will together the number of each ten and each unit to find the code for the tens column we would get:

The first three have nothing in the tens column so we will start with the fourth one.

If we add the two figures of 12 (1 + 2) The answer is 3.

We already have 2 in the units column- so what do we add to 2 to make 3- well 1. So the one goes into the tens column.

eg:

1	2

Similarly 6 is next in the units column. What do we add to 6 to make 7. Well 1 again so we put it in the tens column again.

eg:

1	6

Next 0 is in the units column. What do we add to 0 to make 2- well 2 so put it in the tens column in front of the 0

eg:

2	0

0 4 8 3 7 2 6 1 5 9 4

eg: 9 X 4 = 36
3 + 6 = 9

Cover up what you have just done and see if you can fill in the answers:

0 X 4 =

1 X 4 =

2 X 4 =

3 X 4 =

4 X 4 =

5 X 4 =

6 X 4 =

7 X 4 =

8 X 4 =

9 X 4 =

10 X 4 =

Revision

Lastly we'll do a bit of revision to see how much we have remembered. If you need a bit of help do it the Japanese way:

2 X 4 =	4 X 4 =	0 X 4 =	1 X 4 =	3 X 4 =
6 X 4 =	9 X 4 =	7 X 4 =	5 X 4 =	10 X 4 =
8 X 2 =	9 X 4 =	6 X 4 =	7 X 4 =	3 X 4 =

Turn to the back of the book to mark your answers and see how many you got right … celebrate your success!

The 3 Times Table

The three times table is the first **odd** number table we will tackle together. As before, we will work out the numbers by following the Japanese method counting the crosses.

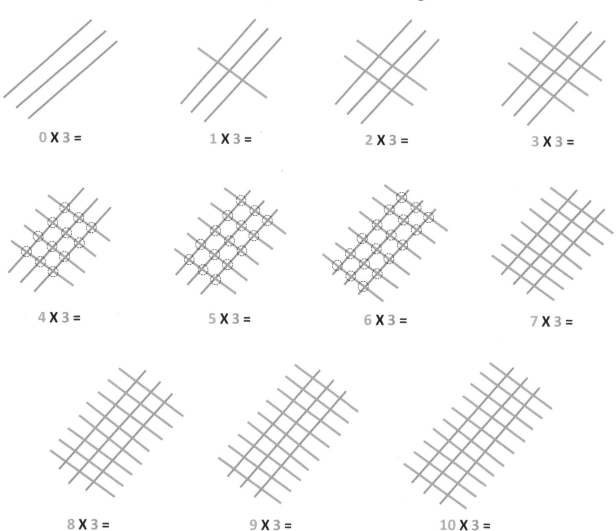

0 X 3 =   1 X 3 =   2 X 3 =   3 X 3 =

4 X 3 =   5 X 3 =   6 X 3 =   7 X 3 =

8 X 3 =   9 X 3 =   10 X 3 =

Now, let's fill in all the answers to the table as we did before.

0 X 3 =

1 X 3 =

2 X 3 =

3 X 3 =

4 X 3 =

5 X 3 =

6 X 3 =

7 X 3 =

8 X 3 =

9 X 3 =

10 X 3 =

Can you see that it looks completely different to the two **even** number tables that we looked at earlier on? Although there is no obvious pattern with the units column, if you look closely you will see another unexpected pattern appear.

Look at the first three numbers after zero: 3, 6 and 9. These numbers will set the pattern of each of the three sets to follow.

$$0 \times 3 = 0$$

$$1 \times 3 = 3$$

$$2 \times 3 = 6$$

$$3 \times 3 = 9$$

$$4 \times 3 = 12$$

$$5 \times 3 = 15$$

$$6 \times 3 = 18$$

$$7 \times 3 = 21$$

$$8 \times 3 = 24$$

$$9 \times 3 = 27$$

$$10 \times 3 = 30$$

When we add up the   1 + 2 of (12) we get 3
1 + 5 of (15) we get 6
1 + 8 of (18) we get 9

Now you can try to fill in the rest of the answers following the same pattern:

$$2 + 1 =$$

$$2 + 4 =$$

$$2 + 7 =$$

$$3 + 0 =$$

Can you see that by adding together the two digits of your original answer that the numbers follow the same pattern again?

Lets now do a bit of revision to see how much we can remember. If you get stuck, don't worry – you can always count the crosses using the Japanese method if you need to.

These questions are not as easy as I have muddled up the order the trick is to start at zero and work your way through it in the normal order.

$$2 \ X \ 3 =$$
$$4 \ X \ 3 =$$
$$0 \ X \ 3 =$$
$$1 \ X \ 3 =$$
$$3 \ X \ 3 =$$
$$6 \ X \ 3 =$$
$$9 \ X \ 3 =$$
$$7 \ X \ 3 =$$
$$5 \ X \ 3 =$$
$$2 \ X \ 3 =$$
$$8 \ X \ 3 =$$
$$10 \ X \ 3 =$$
$$9 \ X \ 3 =$$
$$1 \ X \ 3 =$$
$$7 \ X \ 3 =$$

Revision

As before- we'll do a bit of revision to see how much we have remembered. If you get stuck. Don't forget to count the crosses and use the 3 6 9 code when the need arises:

(a) 2 X 3 =   (b) 4 X 3 =   (c) 0 X 3 =   (d) 1 X 3 =

(e) 3 X 3 =   (f) 6 X 3 =   (g) 9 X 3 =   (h) 7 X 3 =

(i) 5 X 3 =   (j) 2 X 3 =   (k) 8 X 3 =   (l) 10 X 3 =

Turn to the back of the book to mark your answers and see how many you got right … celebrate your success!

The Five times table

As usual, the Japanese method shows us a clear pattern for the units column

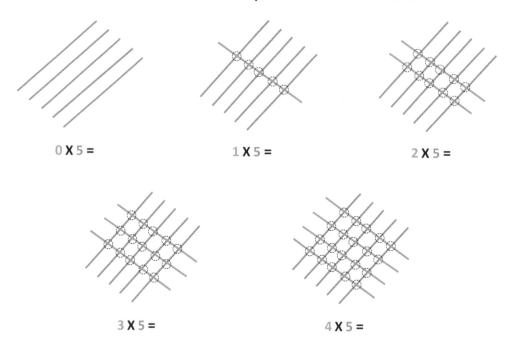

0 X 5 =

1 X 5 =

2 X 5 =

3 X 5 =

4 X 5 =

Count the number of times the lines cross and write in the answers. You will note that the pattern for the units column is always ... followed by ....

Lets now fill in the 5 time table answers and see if they also make a pattern:

$$0 \times 5 = 0$$
$$1 \times 5 = 5$$
$$2 \times 5 = 10$$
$$3 \times 5 = 15$$
$$4 \times 5 = 20$$
$$5 \times 5 = 25$$

We are lucky with this one. Both codes are already done for us. The pattern for the units column is always a ..... followed by a ......' The pattern for the tens is two zeros, two ones and two twos and so on up to five.

Now look at the pattern of the tens column above. That's right – it works in doubles! There were two zeros, two ones and two twos, so you should find it easy to fill in the rest of the pattern now.

$$6 \times 5 =$$
$$7 \times 5 =$$
$$8 \times 5 =$$
$$9 \times 5 =$$
$$10 \times 5 =$$

Look at what happens with multiplying by **odd** or **even** numbers.

When 5 is multiplied by an **even** number such as **2** x 5 or **4** x 5. The answer in the tens column is always **half** of the number you were multiplying by 5. So half of 6 is 3 - put that in the Tens column above.

Now have a look back at the pattern we made by adding up the figures in the tens and units columns above.

That's right! The unit pattern is:

0   5   1   6   2   7   3   8   4   9   5

Now let's use the two codes to fill in the answers by each equals sign.

0 X 5 =

1 X 5 =

2 X 5 =

3 X 5 =

4 X 5 =

5 X 5 =

6 X 5 =

7 X 5 =

8 X 5 =

9 X 5 =

10 X 5 =

If we think back to before, we have already found that the tens column is **half** the number we are multiplying by. So we look at **8** x **5** and the tens column will be **half** of **8**. To make it even easier to follow a pattern, look at how the **odd** number following it will always be the same.

Revision

As before, let's now try a few examples jumbled up to see how we get on:

2 X 5 =	4 X 5 =	0 X 5 =	1 X 5 =	3 X 5 =
6 X 5 =	9 X 5 =	7 X 5 =	5 X 5 =	6 X 3 =
8 X 5 =	10 X 5 =	9 X 5 =	4 X 5 =	7 X 5 =

You are getting seriously good at this now! Go to the back of the book and see how many you got right.

The 10 times Table

The five times was easy but this one is even easier.

Once again we will look at the first five of this table to spot the pattern. Count the crosses and fill in the answers so that we see the pattern.

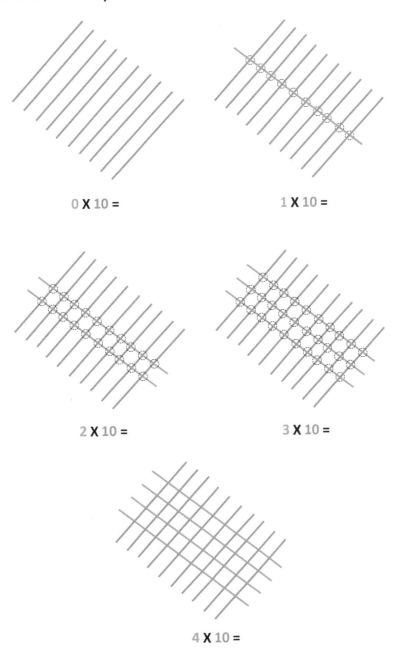

0 X 10 =

1 X 10 =

2 X 10 =

3 X 10 =

4 X 10 =

2 5

You will see from your answers that the patterns for both the units and the tens column are really easy because all the units column end in ...... and the tens column are all the numbers up to ......

0 X 10 =

1 X 10 =

2 X 10 =

3 X 10 =

4 X 10 =

5 X 10 =

6 X 10 =

7 X 10 =

8 X 10 =

9 X 10 =

10 X 10 =

You will see from your answers that the patterns for both the units and tens columns are really easy because all of the answers in the units column end in ☐ and those in the tens column are all the numbers from ☐ to ☐

Now try to cover up the one we have just looked at and tackle the whole table again by yourself.

Revision

0 X 10 =

1 X 10 =

2 X 10 =

3 X 10 =

4 X 10 =

5 X 10 =

6 X 10 =

7 X 10 =

8 X 10 =

9 X 10 =

10 X 10 =

Now for a spot of muddled-up revision again:

6 X 10 =   1 X 10 =   4 X 10 =

1 X 10 =   7 X 10 =   9 X 10 =

3 X 10 =   8 X 10 =   0 X 10 =

4 X 10 =   5 X 10 =   10 X 10 =

I bet you found this one easy! Go to the back of the book and mark them right.

6 Times Table

Once again we will count up, using the Japanese method where each line crosses with circles around them

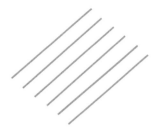

0 X 6 =

1 X 6 =

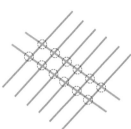

2 X 6 =

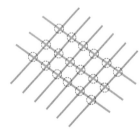

3 X 6 =

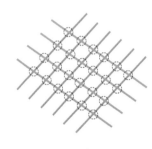

4 X 6 =

Can you fill in the answers to the first five on the table below?

0 X 6 =
1 X 6 =
2 X 6 =
3 X 6 =
4 X 6 =

This gives us a pattern: 0 6 2 8 4

This time make your thumb the zero, first finger 6, middle finger 2, ring finger 8 and your little finger 4. Now close your hand and open it up one at a time saying 0, 6, 2, 8, 4. Do this several times, then you'll remember it easily.

Now let's go back to the Japanese method and count the crosses to fill in the rest of the table:

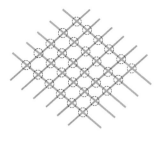

5 X 6 =

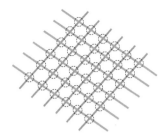

6 X 6 =

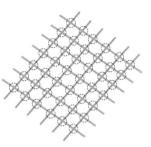

7 X 6 =

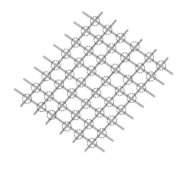

8 X 6 =

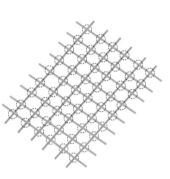

9 X 6 =

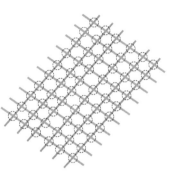

10 X 6 =

5 X 6 =

6 X 6 =

7 X 6 =

8 X 6 =

9 X 6 =

10 X 6 =

Now we will put the two parts together to work out the code for the tens column

$$0 \times 6 = 0$$

$$1 \times 6 = 6$$

$$2 \times 6 = 2$$

$$3 \times 6 = 8$$

$$4 \times 6 = 4$$

$$5 \times 6 = 0$$

$$6 \times 6 = 6$$

$$7 \times 6 = 2$$

$$8 \times 6 = 8$$

$$9 \times 6 = 4$$

$$10 \times 6 = 0$$

We are now up to 3 in the 6 3 9 code. What must we add to the 2 to make it up to 3- one of course. But that 1 needs to go in the tens column in front of the 2.

Now we are up to 9 in the code. The next has 8 in the units column. What must I add to it to make ? It's 1 again- put it in the tens column.

That brings us back to 6 in the code. 4 is in the units column. What must we add to 4 to make 6? It is 2 this time. Put this in the tens column.

This code makes it really easy - you do the rest

Add the two numbers after the zero and we get:

$$6\ 3\ 9\ 6\ 3\ 9\ 6\ 3\ 9\ 6$$

Very much like the three times table. This makes it very easy for us

Put the answers next to each equal sign.

5 X 6 =   6 X 6 =   7 X 6 =   8 X 6 =   9 X 6 =   10 X 6 =

Now cover up the one you have just done and do the same again using both the 0 6 2 8 4 pattern for the units **and the 6 3 9 pattern for the** tens.

There is one problem with the tens column for 8 x 6. The answer 48 is a mystery number. It is the one that the pattern or code will not work for. The 8 is fine in the units column, but the 4 doesn't work for the tens column. The adding up comes out as a 3.

4 + 8 = 12, then 1 + 2 = 3 but there is no way of making a 3 into a 4!

Let's look at this in more detail.

Number of crosses	the 6 3 9 column	finding the tens number
	0	0
	6	6
	3	2
	9	18
	6	24
	3	30
	9	36
	6	42
	3	48
	9	54
	6	60

Now let's look at the one before 48. What do we have to add to 2 to make it 6. Only 4. So the answer is 42.

<u>Revision</u>

Now it is time to see how well you are doing.

2 X 6 =   4 X 6 =   0 X 6 =   1 X 6 =   3 X 6 =

6 X 6 =   9 X 6 =   7 X 6 =   5 X 6 =   6 X 6 =

9 X 6 =   10 X 6 =   8 X 6 =   3 X 6 =   7 X 6 =

One little tip. Say you get stuck on 7 X 6 and can't remember the last figure, you can use your other hand. The first hand has already done up to four. 7 is only three more on, which is the middle finger of the next hand. So just repeat 0, 6, 2 with 2 being the last figure. To work out the tens column use the 6 3 9 code. What number do you add to 2 to make 6? Only 4 does the job and gives an answer of 42.

Brilliant! Give yourself a pat on the back.

8 Times Table

Now we're going to take a look at the eight times table. As before, we will work out the numbers by following the Japanese method counting the crosses and filling in the answers.

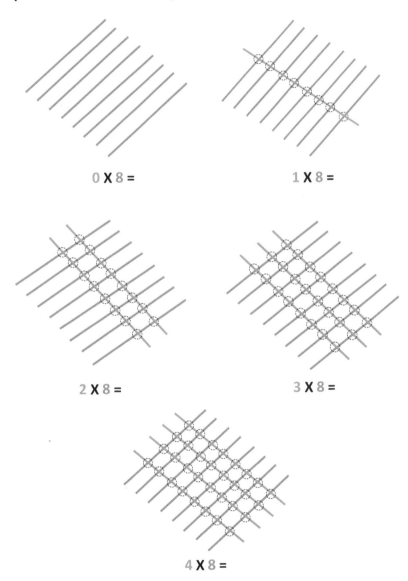

0 X 8 =   1 X 8 =

2 X 8 =   3 X 8 =

4 X 8 =

Counting up the crosses for each one we get: ___ ___ ___ ___ ___ ___. That gives us our pattern of 0 8 6 4 2

A good way to remember this code is to use your best hand. Make your thumb, the zero, the first finger 8. The middle finger 6. The ring finger 4 and the little finger 2. Now close your hand and open it up one at a time saying : 0 8 6 4 2 Do this a few times and you will always remember it.

Write down the answers for the first five:

$$0 \times 8 =$$

$$1 \times 8 =$$

$$2 \times 8 =$$

$$3 \times 8 =$$

$$4 \times 8 =$$

Normally we would need the other Japanese diagrams to work out the code but this one has given us an easier choice. In the units column we have our pattern of 0 8 6 4 2 but now look at what we have in the tens column. All the numbers are climbing upstairs one at a time, except one. You will see what it is when you come to it.

The other clue comes from adding up the two numbers in the answers you have written down. 8 is on its own then comes 16 and 24 etc. They form a pattern of 8 7 6 going all the way downstairs one less at a time.

That's brilliant!   I'll put in the units pattern and leave you to fill in the tens.

Everything goes well until we get to 9 X 8. 8 X 8 comes to 64 , which added together brings us down to 1- so what comes next. The answer is 9 itself. If you look back at some of the tables we have already learned you will find that the two numbers in the answer always add up to 9. So what must we add to 2 to make 9?

There is one more little tip. The number of tens in the answer is usually one less than the number we a multiplying by.

$$5 \times 8 = {-}{-}{-}0$$

$$6 \times 8 = {-}{-}{-}8$$

$$7 \times 8 = {-}{-}{-}6$$

8 X 8 = ---4

9 X 8 = ---2

10 X 8 = ---0

Well done- cover up what you have just done and see what you can remember, using both the 0 8 6 4 2 pattern for the units and the one going upstairs for the tens column:

0 X 8 =

1 X 8 =

2 X 8 =

3 X 8 =

4 X 8 =

5 X 8 =

6 X 8 =

7 X 8 =

8 X 8 =

9 X 8 =

10 X 8 =

Lastly- cover up the one's you have just done- its revision time:

Revision

Don't forget you have the 0 8 6 4 2 code for your two hands, the Japanese way to help you.

(a) 2 X 8 =   (b) 4 X 8 =   (c) 0 X 8 =   (d) 1 x 8 =

(e) 3 X 8 =   (f) 6 X 8 =   (g) 9 X 8 =   (h) 7 X 8 =

(i) 5 x 8 =   (j) 8 X 8 =   (k) 10 X 8 =   (l) 6 X 8 =

Now go to the back of the book and give yourself a pat on the back for getting so many right.

Nine Times Table

Now we're going to take a look at the nine times table. As before, we will work out the numbers by following the Japanese method and counting the crosses. Fetch your pens and paper and complete the answers below.

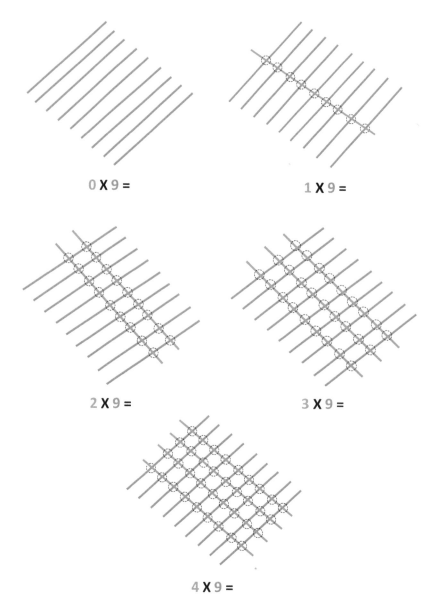

0 X 9 =

1 X 9 =

2 X 9 =

3 X 9 =

4 X 9 =

First count up the crosses for the first five and fill in your answers to see what pattern we get:

$$0 \times 9 = 0$$

$$1 \times 9 = 9$$

$$2 \times 9 = 18$$

$$3 \times 9 = 27$$

$$4 \times 9 = 36$$

That's good! We can see from the first five that the numbers in the units column go downstairs- one at a time from nine- and the tens column go upstairs one at a time.

These numbers give us the pattern we need. It should be easy to fill in the missing ones below. There is also one further clue. The figures of each answer all add up to _____.

$$5 \times 9 =$$

$$6 \times 9 =$$

$$7 \times 9 =$$

$$8 \times 9 =$$

$$9 \times 9 =$$

$$10 \times 9 =$$

Next, cover up what you have just done and complete the table below.

$$0 \times 9 =$$

$$1 \times 9 =$$

$$2 \times 9 =$$

$$3 \times 9 =$$

$$4 \times 9 =$$

$$5 \times 9 =$$

$$6 \times 9 =$$

$$7 \times 9 =$$

$$8 \times 9 =$$

$$9 \times 9 =$$

$$10 \times 9 =$$

Excellent- now it is revision time.

Remember that not only do the units come downstairs one at a time, whilst the tens do the same thing going upwards. There is one further piece of help. Have you noticed that the number of tens is always one less than the one it is multiplied by and as we learned from the 8 times table, when 9 is involved the two numbers in the answer always add up to 9. For example 6 X 9. One less than 6 is 5. And 4 is the number that makes the two numbers add up to 9. So the answer is 54.

(a) 2 X 9 =   (b) 4 X 9 =   (c) 0 X 9 =   (d) 1 x 9 =

(e) 3 X 9 =   (f) 6 X 9 =   (g) 9 X 9 =   (h) 7 X 9 =

(i) 5 X 9 =   (j) 4 X 9 =   (k) 8 X 9 =   (l) 10 X 9 =

I think you will do well with this one. Go to the back of the book and mark it.

The Seven Times Table

Lastly we come to the 7 times table. I left it until last because it is the most difficult and unlike all the others-not to worry! We will have learnt most of the seven times table from the tables we have already done simply because they all have a 7 in them.

A good example is 2 X 7 and 7 X 2

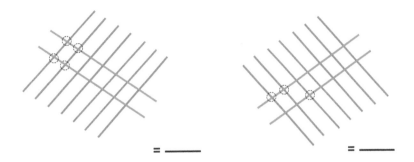

Count up the number of crosses in each. What do you find:

Each has ... ... crosses.

The only one we have not come across in our other tables yet is the 7 X 7 = ... which we will do now.

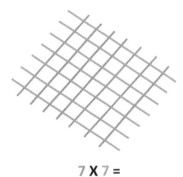

7 X 7 =

Now we will recreate the 7 times tables from what we have learned before. You can either see how many you remember. If you have forgotten any you can draw your own Japanese diagram lines and count the crosses

0 X 7 =

1 X 7 =

2 X 7 =

3 X 7 =

4 X 7 =

5 X 7 =

6 X 7 =

7 X 7 =

8 X 7 =

9 X 7 =

10 X 7 =

That's brilliant! You have now learned all the tables this new way up to ten.

If you like you can skip the next few pages and go on to the revision at the end before going on to numbers greater than ten.

But if you are a hero and would like to discover the secrets of the codes that gives rise to the 7 times tables, cary straight on.

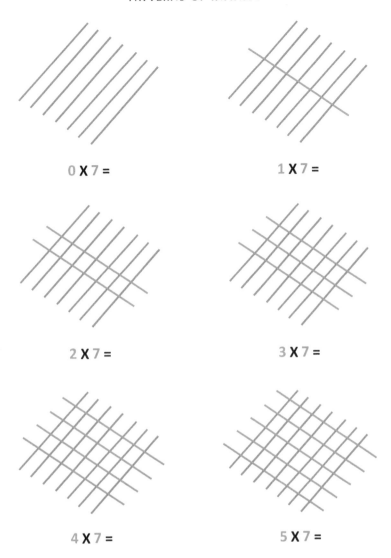

0 X 7 =   1 X 7 =

2 X 7 =   3 X 7 =

4 X 7 =   5 X 7 =

As usual count the crosses and give the answer to each one and then put them in the five below:

0 X 7 =

1 X 7 =

2 X 7 =

3 X 7 =

4 X 7 =

5 X 7 =

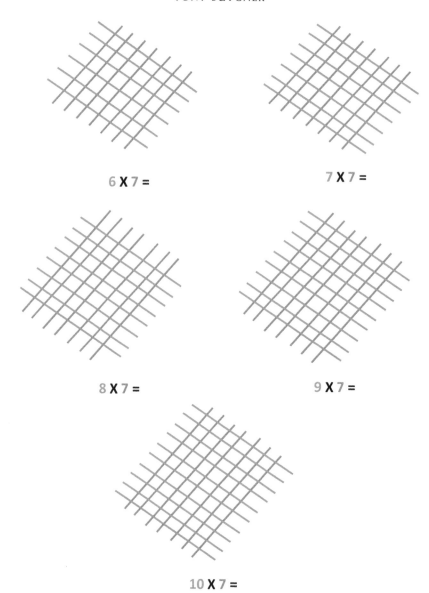

6 X 7 =

7 X 7 =

8 X 7 =

9 X 7 =

10 X 7 =

Now do the same for these

6 X 7 =

7 X 7 =

8 X 7 =

9 X 7 =

10 X 7 =

Do you see what I mean? When first looked at the first five, there seemed to be no pattern for the last column at all. There is one but it is hidden! See if you can you spot it

It is a secret code that would work for all of the tables but the ones we use are much easier to spot and use.

To use this code, as the first number is always 0, we must think of it as – just the home of all numbers. When you put a 1 in front of it and treat it as a ten then take the number of the table away from it, it gives us the code for the units column.

So if we take away 7 from 10 this will help us to easily work out the units column for the 7 times table.

Now we'll work them all out. So it is easy to work out the units column by taking 3 from the number above it. We will do the first three together:

10 – 3 = 7   7 – 3 =   4 – 3 =

Now you do the rest but don't forget if the first number is smaller than the one you are taking away, put a ten in front of it.

So the next one will be 11 – 3.

1 – 3 =   8 – 3 =   5 – 3 =   2 – 3 =

9 – 3 =   6 – 3 =   3 – 3 =

So if we forget this table, we can easily get back the units column by taking away 3 from the number above. Since the first number is zero take it as 10, then we can easily work out the rest of the units

Once again we get the second pattern by adding the numbers of the answer together:

0 + 7 =   1 + 4 =   2 + 1 =   2 + 6 =

3 + 5 =   4 + 2 =   4 + 9 =   5 + 9 =

6 + 3 =   7 + 0 =   7 + 9 =   8 + 8 =

Do you see what we get? That's right. The same two sequences of odd and even numbers we met right with the two times table.

The first line will be 7 5 3 1

The second will be   8 6 4 2

The third will be   9 7

The first and third lines are odd numbers and the second line are even numbers.

Now we can put the two lines of numbers together and recreate the 7 times table.

The first two are already done for us:

$$0 \times 7 = 0$$

$$1 \times 7 = 7$$

Starting at 2 times 7 by taking away 3 from 7 we get 4. Now using the pattern of the tens column we see it is 5. What do we have to add to 4 to make 5? 1 of course – so we add a ten in front of the 4:

$$2 \times 7 = 14$$

We'll do one more together. If we take away 3 from 4 we get 1.

The next in the odd number pattern is 3.

What number in the tens column do we have to add to 1 to make 3? That's right it's 2 tens.

So

$$3 \ X \ 7 = 21$$

Now you try the rest.

$$4 \ X \ 7 =$$

$$5 \ X \ 7 =$$

$$6 \ X \ 7 =$$

$$7 \ X \ 7 =$$

$$8 \ X \ 7 =$$

$$9 \ X \ 7 =$$

$$10 \ X \ 7 =$$

Revision:

Don't forget to draw he numbers the Japanese way to help you if you get stuck.

(a) 2 X 7 =   (b) 4 X 7 =   (c) 0 X 7 =   (d) 1 x 7 =

(e) 3 X 7 =   (f) 6 X 7 =   (g) 9 X 7 =   (h) 7 X 7 =

(i) 5 x 7 =   (j) 8 X 7 =   (k) 4 X 7 =   (l) 10 X 7 =

Numbers Greater than Ten

The Japanese way we have used would still work for larger numbers but you would waste quite a lot of time drawing them and soon get fed up with counting all the crosses, especially as we are now up to larger numbers like the 11 and 12 times tables.

Just a small change to the system makes this much easier. It is the introduction of the tens line, which we will do in orange. We have only done the tables up to 10- now we are going to take them up to 12. We'll start with the two and three times tables.

First I'll show you how the 11 and 12 look:

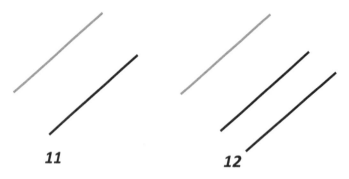

11

12

For 11 the orange line stands for 10 and the one black line for 1.

For 12 the orange line stands for one 10 and the two black lines for 2.

And the two black lines are two units and the black line stands for 1.

Now we will finish off the end of the two times table: Whenever a black line crosses an orange put in a small 10. Also whenever a black line crosses another insert a small 1

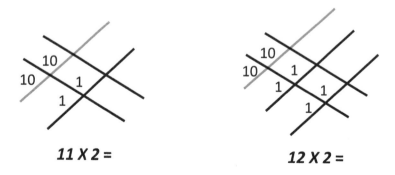

11 X 2 =

12 X 2 =

Whenever a black line crosses an orange line it is worth 10.

In the first we have two black lines crossing the orange 10, which gives us 20. Also two black lines crossing another. Each is worth one unit which gives us 2.

So 20 + 2 = 22

In the second example we have 2 black lines crossing over the orange ten line, which gives us 10 + 10. As before the first two black lines cross the bottom giving 4.

So 12 X 2 = 24.

Now would be a good time to revise the whole table using the two patterns we have now discovered, especially the 0 2 4 6 8 for the units column:

0 X 2 =

1 X 2 =

2 X 2 =

3 X 2 =

4 X 2 =

5 X 2 =

6 X 2 =

7 X 2 =

8 X 2 =

9 X 2 =

10 X 2 =

11 X 2 =

12 X 2 =

Revision

(a) 4 X 2 =   (b) 7 X 2 =   (c) 6 X 2 =   (d) 3 x 2 =   (e) 11 X 2 =

(f) 2 X 2 =   (g) 12 X 2 =   (h) 0 X 2 =   (i) 5 x 2 =   (j) 1 X 2 =

(k) 8 X 2 =   (l) 10 X 2 =   (m) 9 X 2 =

That's very good!

Now we will finish off the 3 times table and revise it in the same way:

Put in a small ten in both diagrams where the black lines cross an orange line and also a small one wherever two black lines cross.

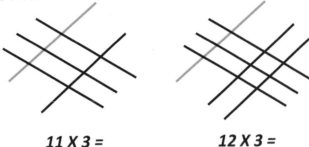

$11 X 3 =$ $12 X 3 =$

One more example. The orange line is crossed by three black ones making 30. They also cross the 1 black line making 3 more. Making 33.

As before we will now revise the whole table adding the last two on the end but don't forget its 3 6 9 pattern:

0 X 3 =

1 X 3 =

2 X 3 =

3 X 3 =

4 X 3 =

5 X 3 =

6 X 3 =

7 X 3 =

8 X 3 =

9 X 3 =

10 X 3 =

11 X 3 =

12 X 3 =

<u>Revision</u>

(a) 3 X 3 =   (b) 6 X 3 =   (c) 9 X 3 =   (d) 4 x 3 =   (e) 11 X 3 =

(f) 2 X 3 =   (g) 8 X 3 =   (h) 12 X 3 =   (i) 0 x 3 =   (j) 7 X 3 =

(k) 10 X 3 =   (l) 5 X 3 =   (m) 1 X 3 =

Finish off the 4 times table and then revise:

Put in a small ten in both diagrams where the black lines cross an orange line and also a small one wherever two black lines cross.

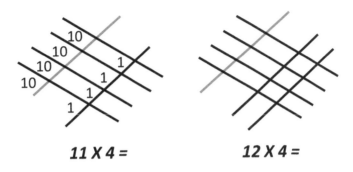

11 X 4 =   *12 X 4 =*

I have put in the 10's and 1's in 11 x 4 you do the same for 12 X 4.

Remember that the units code is 0 4 8 2 6 and the tens column is 0 4 8 3 7 2 6 1 5 9 4

0 X 4 =

1 X 4 =

2 X 4 =

3 X 4 =

4 X 4 =

5 X 4 =

6 X 4 =

7 X 4 =

8 X 4 =

9 X 4 =

10 X 4 =

11 X 4 =

12 X 4 =

Revision

(a) 2 X 4 =   (b) 7 X 4 =   (c) 0 X 4 =   (d) 5 X 4 =   (e) 6 X 4 =

(f) 1 X 4 =   (g) 3 X 4 =   (h) 8 X 4 =   (i) 10 X 4 =   (j) 4 X 4 =

(k) 9 X 4 =   (l) 11 X 4 =   (m) 12 X 4 =

Well done- go to the back of the book and mark them.

That's very good!

Finish off the 5 times table and then revise:

Put in your own 10's and 1's in these two to make them easier.

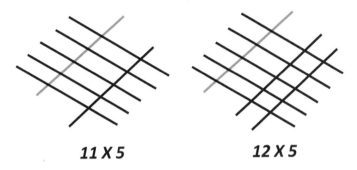

11 X 5   *12 X 5*

Remember that the pattern for the units column is 0 and 5 and the tens column goes up in twos-like two zeros, two ones , two twos etc.

0 X 5 =

1 X 5 =

2 X 5 =

3 X 5 =

4 X 5 =

5 X 5 =

6 X 5 =

7 X 5 =

8 X 5 =

9 x 5 =

10 X 5 =

11 X 5 =

12 X 5 =

<u>Revision</u>

(a) 3 X 5 =   (b) 6 X 5 =   (c) 8 X 5 =   (d) 10 X 5 =   (e) 0 X 5 =

(f) 1 X 5 =   (g) 5 X 5 =   (h) 2 X 5 =   (i) 4 X 5 =   (j) 11 X 5 =

(k) 12 X 5 =   (l) 7 X 5 =   (m) 9 X 5 =

Finish off the 6 times table and then revise:

Write a small 10 or 1 whenever the lines cross.

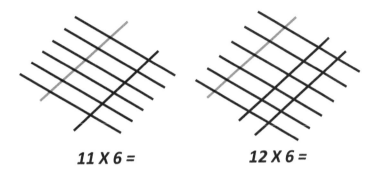

11 X 6 =   *12 X 6 =*

Don't forget to put the 0 6 2 8 4 in the units column first and use the 6 3 9 code after the zero for the tens.

0 X 6 =

1 X 6 =

2 X 6 =

3 X 6 =

4 X 6 =

5 X 6 =

6 X 6 =

7 X 6 =

8 X 6 =

9 X 6 =

10 X 6 =

11 X 6 =

12 X 6 =

<u>Revision</u>

(a) 8 X 6 =   (b) 12 X 6 =   (c) 1 X 6 =   (d) 4 X 6 =   (e) 0 X 6 =

(f) 5 X 6 =   (g) 9 X 6 =   (h) 3 X 6 =   (i) 10 X 6 =   (j) 6 X 6 =

(k) 2 X 6 =   (l) 7 X 6 =   (m) 11 X 6 =

Brilliant- go to the back of the book and see how many ticks you get.

Finish off the 8 times table and then revise:

As before, if it helps put a small ten whenever a black line crosses an orange one and also when one or more black lines cross.

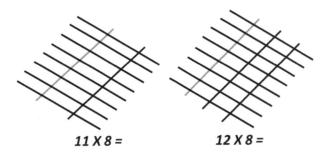

11 X 8 =   12 X 8 =

First put in our units column pattern of 0 8 6 4 2 but now look at what we have in the tens column. All the numbers we have written down are climbing upstairs one at a time, except one. You will see what it is when you come to it.

The other clue comes from adding up the two numbers in the answers you have written down. 8 is on its own then comes 16 and 24 etc. They form a pattern of 8 7 6 going all the way downstairs one less at a time.

0 X 8 =

1 X 8 =

2 X 8 =

3 X 8 =

4 X 8 =

5 X 8 =

6 X 8 =

7 X 8 =

8 X 8 =

9 X 8 =

10 X 8 =

11 X 8 =

12 X 8 =

Revision

(a) 0 X 8 =   (b) 4 X 8 =   (c) 7 X 8 =   (d) 3 X 8 =   (e) 5 X 8 =

(f) 6 X 8 =   (g) 9 X 8 =   (h) 2 X 8 =   (i) 8 X 8 =   (j) 1 X 8 =

(k) 10 X 8 =   (l) 12 X 8 =   (m) 11 X 8 =

That's brilliant- go to the back and mark them.

Finish off the 7 times table and then revise:

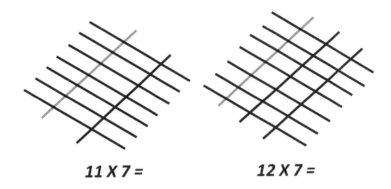

11 X 7 =   12 X 7 =

Remember that whenever the first figure is smaller than 7 add a ten to make it possible to take 7 from it to find the units code.

0 X 7 =   0

1 X 7 =

2 X 7 =

3 X 7 =

4 X 7 =

5 X 7 =

6 X 7 =

7 X 7 =

8 X 7 =

9 X 7 =

10 X 7 =

11 X 7 =

12 X 7 =

Revision

(a) 3 X 7 =   (b) 7 X 7 =   (c) 4 X 7 =   (d) 6 X 7 =   (e) 1 X 7 =

(f) 2 X 7 =   (g) 9 X 7 =   (h) 11 X 7 =   (i) 8 X 7 =   (j) 5 X 7 =

(k) 10 X 7 =   (l) 12 X 7 =   (m) 10 X 7 =

Well done! Go to the back of the book and mark them.

The 9 Times Table

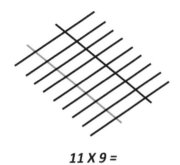

11 X 9 =

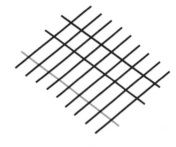

12 X 9 =

This is a nice easy one to fill in and then revise:

0 X 9 =

1 X 9 =

2 X 9 =

3 X 9 =

4 X 9 =

5 X 9 =

6 X 9 =

7 X 9 =

8 X 9 =

9 X 9 =

10 X 9 =

11 X 9 =

12 X 9 =

Revision

(a) 2 X 9 =   (b) 5 X 9 =   (c) 7 X 9 =   (d) 9 x 9 =   (e) 3 X 9 =

(f) 1 X 9 =   (g) 9 X 9 =   (h) 11 X 9 =   (i) 8 x 9 =   (j) 5 X 9 =

(k) 10 X 9 =   (l) 12 X 9 =   (m) 10 X 9 =

Well done! Go to the back of the book and mark them.

The 10 Times Table

Making even larger numbers simple

When both numbers are 10 or larger than 10 we need another ten line.

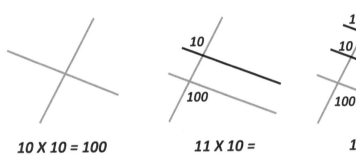

10 X 10 = 100   11 X 10 =   12 X 10 =

This must be the easiest one of all. The units column is always zero and the tens are always the same as each ten is multiplied by.

$$0 \ X \ 10 \ =$$

$$1 \ X \ 10 \ =$$

$$2 \ X \ 10 \ =$$

$$3 \ X \ 10 \ =$$

$$4 \ X \ 10 \ =$$

$$5 \ X \ 10 \ =$$

$$6 \ X \ 10 \ =$$

$$7 \ X \ 10 \ =$$

$$8 \ X \ 10 \ =$$

$$9 \ X \ 10 \ =$$

$$10 \ X \ 10 \ =$$

$$11 \ X \ 10 \ =$$

$$12 \ X \ 10 \ =$$

Revision

(a) 8 X 10 =   (b) 12 X 10 =   (c) 1 X 10 =   (d) 4 x 10 =   (e) 0 X 10 =

(f) 5 X 10 =   (g) 9 X 10 =   (h) 3 X 10 =   (i) 10 x 10 =   (j) 6 X 10 =

(k) 2 X 10 =   (l) 7 X 10 =   (m) 11 X 10 =

Well done!

I think they are all straight forward.

The next three will be needed soon. They are a little more detailed so I will show you how it works.

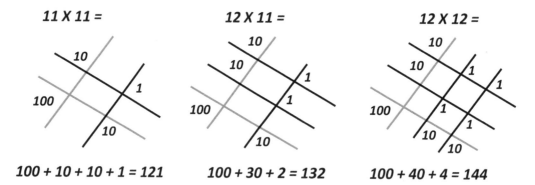

In all three diagrams there are two orange lines. Where they cross we have 10 X 10 which is 100.

When an orange line crosses a black one we get 10. This happens twice. One at the top and one at the bottom , which makes 20.

Finally when two black lines cross we get 1.

So altogether we have 100 + 20 + 1= 121.

They do look a bit of a handful at first. Take it slowly. I am sure you will get the hang of it.

The 11 Times Table

First we will look at the first few to get the pattern. Count the crosses and write down what you get.

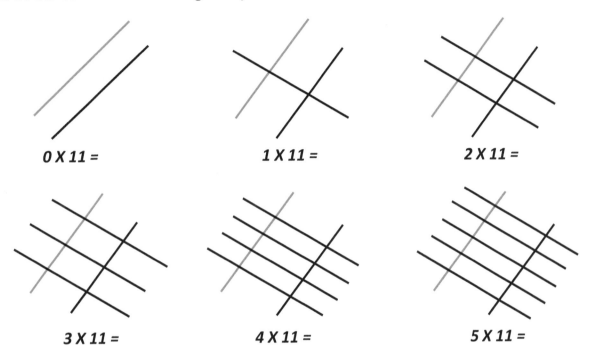

0 X 11 =   1 X 11 =   2 X 11 =

3 X 11 =   4 X 11 =   5 X 11 =

Put your answers in the table below:

0 X 11 =

1 X 11 =

2 X 11 =

3 X 11 =

4 X 11 =

5 X 11 =

What do you notice? That both the units column and the tens go up one at a time after the zero. Also up to nine both the tens and the units are the same number they are multiplied by, so 5 X 11 = 55.

Now fill in the rest.

$$6 \times 11 =$$

$$7 \times 11 =$$

$$8 \times 11 =$$

$$9 \times 11 =$$

Remember the answers to the next three are given by the examples in *Something to Make Even Larger Numbers Simple.*

$$10 \times 11 =$$

$$11 \times 11 =$$

$$12 \times 11 =$$

The units column goes from _____ to _____.

And the tens column does the same thing except when it gets to 10 it jumps one from _____ to _____ then it begins all over again.

The pattern of the tens column is:

—— —— —— —— —— —— —— —— —— —— —— ——

The pattern of numbers of each answer go like this:

—— —— —— —— —— —— —— —— —— —— —— ——

You have seen this one before. Can you remember which table had the same pattern for the last column?

Now fill in the answers using whatever method you prefer.

1 X 11 =

2 X 11 =

3 X 11 =

4 X 11 =

5 X 11 =

6 X 11 =

7 X 11 =

8 X 11 =

9 X 11 =

10 X 11 =

11 X 11 =

12 X 11 =

Revision

1 X 11 =	4 X 11 =	0 X 11 =	6 X 11 =	3 X 11 =
2 X 11 =	9 X 11 =	7 X 11 =	5 X 11 =	12 X 11 =
9 X 11 =	10 X 11 =	8 X 11 =	11 X 11 =	7 X 11 =

Great- now go to the back of the book to see how many you got right.

The 12 Times Table

Count the crosses and fill in the answers. You may find a couple of surprises.

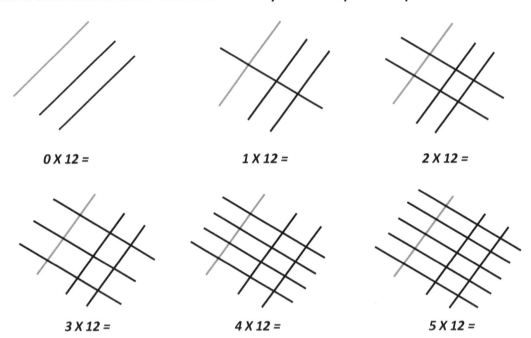

0 X 12 =	1 X 12 =	2 X 12 =

3 X 12 =	4 X 12 =	5 X 12 =

Now fill in the spaces below to see the pattern.

0 X 12 =

1 X 12 =

2 X 12 =

3 X 12 =

4 X 12 =

What do you notice? That's right it is 0 2 4 6 8 the same as the 2 times table. Also if you add up the figures in the answer after the zero the pattern is .... the same as the 3 times table.

The two figures of 48 add up to 12, so we add these two figures and end up with 3, so we know that the next two figures add up to 6 What is the next higher number that adds up to 6? That's right a 6 and a 0 to make 60.

5 X 12 =

6 X 12 =

7 X 12 =

8 X 12 =

9 X 12 =

10 X 12 =

11 X 12 =

12 X 12 =

Don't forget that the answers of the last three are already done or you in the examples of *Something to Make Even Larger Numbers Simple*, which we did earlier.

Now it is time to cover up the one we have just done and fill in the answers to the one below. Best of luck!

Just a reminder- the units column is the same as the two times and the two or three numbers of each answer added together has the 3   6   9 pattern of the three times table.

0 X 12 =

1 X 12 =

2 X 12 =

3 X 12 =

4 X 12 =

5 X 12 =

6 X 12 =

7 X 12 =

8 X 12 =

9 X 12 =

10 X 12 =

11 X 12 =

12 X 12 =

Revision

1 X 12 =	4 X 12 =	0 X 12 =	3 X 12 =	1 X 12 =
6 X 12 =	9 X 12 =	7 X 12 =	5 X 12 =	12 X 12 =
9 X 12 =	11 X 12 =	8 X 12 =	11 X 12 =	7 X 12 =

That's brilliant- well done! I am very proud of you. You have finished them all. Go to the back of the book to mark them. Only do the next few pages if you really want to.

Long Multiplication

The reason we have to learn tables is to do multiplication sums. It is best to stick to the way they teach you at school but it is always useful to have another way to check your answer.

The Japanese way we have used so far only works for answers under 100. It would still work for larger numbers but you would soon get fed up with counting all the crosses.

Just a small change to the system makes this much easier. It is the introduction of the tens line. Instead of drawing ten lines, which are crossed over by four more and counting up to 40 there is just one 'tens line' in orange, which is crossed over by four others. Have a look at this and the next two. See how they are set out. I will be giving you a few to do yourself.

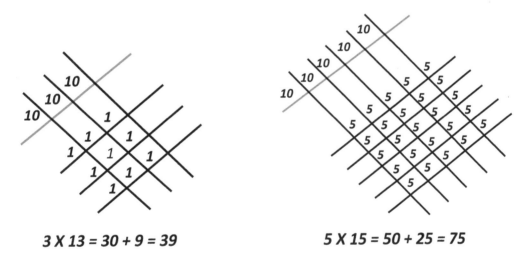

3 X 13 = 30 + 9 = 39   5 X 15 = 50 + 25 = 75

As you can see from the first one, the three lines crossing the ten line gives us 30 and also 9 more when the other black lines cross each other.

In the second example the five lines crossing the ten line and the five others, gives us: 50 + 25= 75.

Why not use the way they show you at school and check the answers the Japanese way for the following:

Revision

(1) 5 X 16 =   (2) 7 X 13 =   (3) 0 X 13 =   (4) 4 X 14 =

(5) 4 X 21 =   (6) 3 X 31 =   (7) 7 X 14 =   (8) 2 X 45 =

Now go to the Answers page to check that you have got them right.

The next few examples show you how to set out the sums when both numbers are more than ten. This one is 41 X 13 =

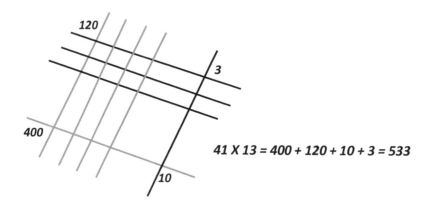

41 X 13 = 400 + 120 + 10 + 3 = 533

The orange and the purple lines are both 10's so where they cross is worth 100. Where the other lines cross a 10 line, each one is worth 10. As you can see there are 12 lots of 10 at the top and one at the bottom. The other lines that cross each other are only worth 1 each.

So if we put together all the numbers for 41 X 13 we get:

400 + 120 + 10 + 3 = 533

Have a look at two more examples to see how it works each time:

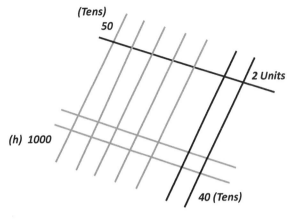

52 X 21 = 1000 + 50 + 40 + 2 = 1092

24 X 11 =

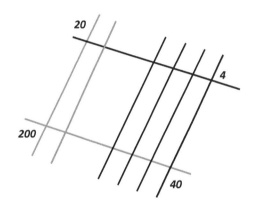

In this one 2 lots of 100. 2 tens at the top and 4 at the bottom. And 4 ones.

That gives us: 200 + 40 + 20 + 4 = 264

24 X 11= 264

Now have a go at some yourself. It is easier to draw them but you could use straws or lolly sticks.

(9) 52 X 12 =   **(10)** 24 X 11 =   **(11)** 41 X 13 =   **(12)** 22 X 14 =

(13) 36 X 15 =   **(14)** 28 X 13 =   **(15)** 32 X 22 =   **(16)** 41 X 24 =

(17) 31 X 31 =   **(18)** 42 X 15 =   **(19)** 21 X 30 =   **(20)** 16 X 15 =

Have a look at the Answers page to see if you have got them right.

Revision Answers

Practice Page

The first four are less than 10 and the next few are between 10 and 18.

(a) 2 X 2 = 4   (b) 4 X 2 = 8   (c) 0 X 2 = 0   (d) 1 X 2 = 2   (e) 3 X 2 = 6

(f) 6 X 2 = 12   (g) 4 X 2 = 8   (h) 7 X 2 = 14   (i) 5 X 2 = 10   (j) 3 x 2 = 6

(k) 8 x 2 = 16   (l) 2 X 2 = 4   (m) 9 X 2 = 18   (n) 1 X 2 = 2   (o) 7 X 2 = 14

Let's do a few more to help you remember. You may find it easier to draw the lines for each numbers and count how many times they cross. When you draw them, think of the number on a clock. The lines for the table itself goes from 8 to 2 and how many from 10 to 4.

Another way is to use your other hand. Your first hand gives you the last figure up to 4 the other hand will help you with the rest. Imagine you get stuck on 7 X 2. 7 is just three more so the middle figure of your other hand will let you know it is 4

Page 12

(a) 5 X 2 = 10   (b) 7 X 2 = 14   (c) 2 X 2 = 4   (d) 10 X 2 = 20

(e) 8 X 2 = 16   (f) 6 X 2 = 12   (g) 1 X 2 =2   (h) 9 X 2 = 18

(i) 0 x 2 = 0   (j) 3 X 2 = 6   (k) 4 X 2 = 8   (l) 9 X 2 = 18

Page 17

(a) 2 X 4 = 8   (b) 4 X 4 = 16   (c) 0 X 4 = 0   (d) 1 X 4 = 4

(e) 3 X 4 = 12   (f) 6 X 4 = 24   (g) 9 X 4 = 36   (h) 7 X 4 = 28

(i) 5 x 4 = 20   (j) 10 X 4 = 40   (k) 8 X 2 = 16   (l) 9 X 4 = 36

Page 21

(a) 2 X 3 = 6   (b) 4 X 3 = 12   (c) 0 X 3 = 0   (d) 1 X 3 = 3

(e) 3 X 3 = 9   (f) 6 X 3 = 18   (g) 9 X 3 = 27   (h) 7 X 3 = 21

(i) 5 x 3 = 15   (j) 2 X 3 = 6   (k) 8 X 3 = 24   (l) 10 X 3 = 30

Page 24

(a) 2 X 5 = 10   (b) 4 X 5 = 20   (c) 0 X 5 = 0   (d) 1 X 5 = 5

(e) 3 X 5 = 15   (f) 6 X 5 = 30   (g) 9 X 5 = 45   (h) 7 X 5 = 35

(i) 5 x 5 = 25   (j) 6 X 5 = 30   (k) 8 X 5 = 40   (l) 10 X 5 = 50

Page 27

(a) 6 X 10 = 60   (b) 1 X 10 = 10   (c) 4 X 10 = 40   (d) 7 X 10 = 70

(e) 9 X 10 = 90   (f) 3 X 10 = 30   (g) 8 X 10 = 80   (h) 0 X 10 = 0

(i) 2 x 10 = 20   (j) 4 X 10 = 40   (k) 5 X 10 = 50   (l) 10 X 10 = 100

Page 32

(a) 2 X 6 = 12   (b) 4 X 6 = 24   (c) 0 X 6 = 0   (d) 1 X 6 = 6

(e) 3 X 6 = 18   (f) 5 X 6 = 30   (g) 9 X 6 = 54   (h) 10 X 6 = 60

(i) 8 x 6 = 48   (j) 3 X 6 = 18   (k) 7 X 6 = 42   (l) 6 X 6 = 36

Page 35

(a) 2 X 8 = 16   (b) 4 X 8 = 32   (c) 0 X 8 = 0   (d) 1 X 8 = 8

(e) 3 X 8 = 24   (f) 6 X 8 = 48   (g) 9 X 8 = 72   (h) 7 X 8 = 56

(i) 5 x 8 = 40   (j) 8 X 8 = 64   (k) 10 X 8 = 80   (l) 6 X 8 = 48

Page 38

(a) 2 X 9 = 18   (b) 4 X 9 = 36   (c) 0 X 9 = 0   (d) 1 X 9 = 9

(e) 3 X 9 = 27   (f) 6 X 9 = 54   (g) 9 X 9 = 81   (h) 7 X 9 = 63

(i) 5 x 9 = 45   (j) 4 X 9 = 36   (k) 8 X 9 = 72   (l) 10 X 9 = 90

Page 45

(a) 2 X 7 = 14   (b) 4 X 7 = 28   (c) 0 X 7 = 0   (d) 1 X 7 = 7

(e) 3 X 7 = 21   (f) 6 X 7 = 42   (g) 9 X 7 = 63   (h) 7 X 7 = 49

(i) 5 x 7 = 35   (j) 8 X 7 = 56   (k) 4 X 7 = 28   (l) 10 X 7 = 70

Page 48

(a) 4 X 2 =   (b) 7 X 2 =   (c) 6 X 2 =   (d) 3 x 2 =   (e) 11 X 2 =

(f) 2 X 2 =   (g) 12 X 2 =   (h) 0 X 2 =   (i) 5 x 2 =   (j) 1 X 2 =

(k) 8 X 2 =   (l) 10 X 2 =   (m) 9 X 2 =

Page 50

(a) 3 X 3 = 9   (b) 6 X 3 = 18   (c) 9 X 3 = 27   (d) 4 X 3 = 12   (e) 11 X 3 = 33

(f) 2 X 3 = 6   (g) 8 X 3 = 24   (h) 12 X 3 = 36   (i) 0 X 3 = 0   (j) 7 X 3 = 21

(k) 10 X 3 = 30   (l) 5 X 3 = 15   (m) 1 X 3 = 1

Page 52

(a) 2 X 4 = 8   (b) 7 X 4 = 24   (c) 0 X 4 = 0   (d) 5 X 4 = 20   (e) 6 X 3 = 18

(f) 1 X 4 = 4   (g) 3 X 4 = 12   (h) 8 X 4 = 32   (i) 10 X 4 = 40   (j) 4 X 4 = 16

(k) 9 X 4 = 36   (l) 11 X 4 = 44   (m) 12 X 4 = 48

Page 54

(a) 3 X 5 = 15   (b) 6 X 5 = 30   (c) 8 X 5 = 40   (d) 10 X 5 = 50   (e) 0 X 5 = 0

(f) 1 X 5 = 5   (g) 5 X 5 = 25   (h) 2 X 5 = 10   (i) 4 X 5 = 20   (j) 11 X 5 = 55

(k) 12 X 5 = 60   (l) 7 X 5 = 36   (m) 9 X 5 = 45

Page 56

(a) 8 X 6 = 48   (b) 12 X 6 = 72   (c) 1 X 6 = 6   (d) 4 x 6 = 24   (e) 0 X 6 = 0

(f) 5 X 6 = 30   (g) 9 X 6 = 54   (h) 3 X 6 = 18   (i) 10 x 6 = 60   (j) 6 X 6 = 36

(k) 2 X 6 = 12   (l) 7 X 6 = 42   (m) 11 X 6 = 66

Page 58

(a) 0 X 8 = 0   (b) 4 X 8 = 32   (c) 7 X 8 = 56   (d) 3 X 8 = 24   (e) 5 X 8 = 40

(f) 6 X 8 = 48   (g) 9 X 8 = 72   (h) 2 X 8 = 16   (i) 8 X 8 = 64   (j) 1 X 8 = 8

(k) 10 X 8 = 80   (l) 12 X 8 = 96   (m) 11 X 8 = 88

Revision

Page 60

(a) 3 X 7 = 21   (b) 7 X 7 = 49   (c) 4 X 7 = 28   (d) 6 X 7 = 42   (e) 1 X 7 =7

(f) 2 X 7 = 14   (g) 9 X 7 = 83   (h) 11 X 7 = 77   (i) 8 X 7 = 56   (j) 5 X 7 = 35

(k) 10 X 7 = 70   (l) 12 X 7 = 84   (m) 10 X 7 =70

Page 62

(a) 2 X 9 = 18   (b) 5 X 9 = 45   (c) 7 X 9 = 63   (d) 9 X 9 = 81   (e) 3 X 9 = 27

(f) 2 X 9 = 18   (g) 9 X 9 = 81   (h) 11 X 9 = 99   (i) 8 X 9 = 72   (j) 5 X 9 = 45

(k) 10 X 9 = 90   (l) 12 X 9 = 108   (m) 7 X 11 = 77

Page 64

(a) 4 X 10 = 40   (b) 8 X 10 = 80   (c) 3 X 10 = 30   (d) 2 x 10 = 20   (e) 0 X 10 = 0

(f) 5 X 10 = 50   (g) 6 X 10 = 60   (h) 1 X 10 = 10   (i) 9 x 10 = 90   (j) 10 X 10 = 100

(k) 8 X 10 = 80   (l) 12 X 10 = 120   (m) 7 X 10 = 70

Page 67

(a) 1 X 11 = 11   (b) 4 X 11 = 44   (c) 0 X 11 = 0   (d) 6 X 11 = 66

(e) 3 X 11 = 33   (f) 2 X 11 = 22   (g) 9 X 11 = 99   (h) 7 X 11 = 77

(i) 5 x 11 = 55   (j) 12 X 11 = 132   (k) 10 X 11 = 110

(l) 8 x 11 = 88   (m) 11 X 11 = 121   (m) 7 X 11 = 77

Page 70

(a) 2 X 12 = 24   (b) 4 X 12 = 48   (c) 0 X 12 = 0   (d) 3 X 12 = 36

(e) 1 X 12 = 12   (f) 6 X 12 = 72   (g) 9 X 12 = 108   (h) 7 X 12 = 84

(i) 5 x 12 = 60   (j) 12 X 12 = 144   (k) 8 X 12 = 96   (l) 11 X 12 = 132

(1)   80   (2)   91   (3)   65   (4)   56

(5)   84   (6)   93   (7)   56   (8)   90

(9)   624   (10) 264   (11) 533   (12) 308

(13) 540   (14) 364   (15) 704   (16) 984

(17) 961   (18) 630   (19) 420   (20) 240

Lightning Source UK Ltd.
Milton Keynes UK
UKHW021059141021
392149UK00004B/40